LYONEL FEININGER

Feininger   Lüneburg IV   d. 20. Okt. 1923

FELICITAS TOBIEN

LYONEL FEININGER

Artline Editions

Translated by Stephen Gorman

© 1989 by Berghaus Verlag — D-8347 Kirchdorf/Inn
English Language Rights: Artlines UK Ltd, 2 Castle Street, Thornbury, Bristol. Avon, England
Printed in West Germany — Imprimé en Allemagne
ISBN 1 871487 13 7

CONTENTS

"I do not paint to create art: it is a deep, painful, human desire to represent innermost experiences, to emphasize something from the past. Perhaps this is completely wrong: but in the present one only has the creation, the work itself . . . the inspiration is surely in the desire for happiness past . . ."

Lyonel Feininger was a man of quiet tone, of fantastic and poetic representation, more concerned with striking the responsive chord of true sensation in his figurative language than being talked about because of his over-expressionistic use of materials. He regarded himself as having "no pretensions of being a 'modern' artist", but was simply happy to have found "adequate pictorial forms" for himself which enabled him to "express his innermost love and desire" and "to satisfy his need for clarity and space".

Feininger was an individualist like Nolde who always acted on intuition; as well as this he possessed an iron will and strong self-discipline. In everything he did, he always felt himself to be a servant of the work, as it were, he saw the "constant necessity of stepping behind the work". This attitude did not alter during all the years in which he was able to create so successfully. He was disturbed when he discovered signs that others were disregarding this important demand in art. "Exhibitionism in art," he once wrote, "is now in fashion. I, on the other hand, attempt to withdraw myself behind my works . . ."

Lyonel Feininger was born in New York on July 7th, 1871, the son of German-American parents. His father, Charles Feininger, was a famous violinist and composer, his mother, Elisabeth née Lutz, a singer and pianist. The boy grew up in a world full of music, and soon this musical world drew him under its spell, characterized his personality and made him sensitive and receptive for other fields of art. When he was nine years old, Lyonel received his first violin lessons from his father; when he was twelve, he already appeared in concerts. Music belonged to his life as much as the daily bread. "I am incomplete," he commented later, "and one of my senses goes to waste and is tortured when I cannot have any music."

The parents' professions caused them to be absent from home for long periods of time when they were performing on concert tours. Lyonel was then mostly given in care to friends who seemingly did not have the necessary amount of understanding for his exceptional intellectual and musical inclinations.

When he travelled to Germany in autumn 1887, a new period began in his life. He was then sixteen years old and his parents were performing in Berlin as part of a European tour. He left the country of his birth and went to the home of his forefathers which he soon regarded as his home too. Actually he had intended and was meant to continue his violin studies in Leipzig, but no sooner had he reached Germany than a surprising change of mind came over him: he decided to become a painter. Luckily his parents had no objections and allowed him to enrol in the arts-and-crafts school in Hamburg.

In the school's "Easter Exhibition", which took place just a few months after his entry, Feininger was represented with 13 sketches and aroused a great deal of interest in the public. On October 1st, 1888 he passed the entrance examination for the Berlin Academy where he was taught by Ernst Hancke and Woldemar Friedrich.

An exceptional drawing talent with obvious humorous tendencies soon became obvious and this decided the artistic direction which the young Feininger took for a long time. However, it took him away from his true aim, i.e. painting. He became a cartoonist.

In 1889 he already received his first commissions for the "Humoristische Blätter" and the "Berliner Blätter" and also commissions to illustrate short stories. After he had attended the Jesuit college St. Servais in Liège to study French, corresponding to his father's wishes, Feininger returned to Berlin in 1891 and continued his studies for a further year in Adolf Schablitz's studio and in the higher class of ancient art under Professor Woldemar Friedrich. Following this, he spent six months in Paris where he attended the Studio Colarossi.

In Berlin, everyone soon wanted the highly talented cartoonist Feininger, who had in the meantime decided to "flood" the "comic magazines" with his work - a decision which was easy to carry out as there were so few illustrators of his standard.

"Harpers Young People", "Ulk", "Lustige Blätter" and "Narrenschiff" were the names of these humorous magazines which were able to thank Feininger in the following years for numerous caricatures. For a time he had a contract with "Ulk", but he cancelled it when he saw that changes demanded by the publishers threatened to reduce his art to a lower standard and that the cheap printing process could cause damage to his good reputation as a draughtsman.

Even then he had, in spite of his youth, an antenna for doing or not doing what was right for him in decisive moments. With the help of this recipe for success and thanks to his ability he was soon highly regarded. Georg Hermann wrote in 1901 in "The Caricature in the 19th Century": "The main draughtsman in Berlin is Lyonel Feininger; even if there remains in this German-American a trace of Yankeeism, snobbery, a tendency to burlesque exaggeration, an individual typical Berlin-style has formed. Feininger measures up to all tasks, he creates political prints of monumental effect with strong contrasts, . . . he strews a print with small amusing figures, muddled ideas of a playful art of drawing, and at the same time a very individual fairy-tale fantasy of compelling comedy rests within him. He has a profound understanding of everything which is connected with modern machines, technology and ships . . . He has an extraordinary drawing ability, an extraordinary understanding for form. And as his talent, in every way modern, does not represent a tendency in any way, but retains its free, pure artistic outlook, we are able to simply enjoy him."

His occupation as a cartoonist brought Feininger financial security as well as success and was undoubtedly the decisive factor for his remaining true to his profession for so long and denying his love for painting - even to himself - for almost 15 years. Later he frankly admitted that he was artistically not completely happy when he explained, for example, that he had worked as an illustrator "compulsorily, to be able to live" and that he had always "tormented himself terribly to be able to satisfy the publishers' demands to a certain degree."

In 1901 Lyonel Feininger married Clara Fürst, the daughter of Gustav Fürst, the painter. But this marriage, in which two daughters were born, only lasted for a short time. They separated in 1905 and Feininger got to know his future partner in life, Julia

Table I

West-Deep. 1934
Watercolour, 23.8 x 42 cm
K.E. Osthaus Museum, Hagen

Berg. This connection proved to be very harmonious, also in regards to work - Julia was an artist as well. The marriage took place in London in 1908. The first son, Andreas, had already been born in 1906, the sons Lawrence and Theodore Lux were born in 1909 and 1910.

At the time of their meeting, Julia Berg was attending several graphic courses at the Grand Ducal School of Arts-and-Crafts in Weimar. Encouraged by her description of what she learned there, the wish to turn towards graphic art arose in Feininger. "... I have a great desire for lithography ... I also learn etching ... above all, I wish to make a series with motifs such as old cities, and then a locomotive cycle ...," he wrote to her in 1905. Soon after this he made his first three lithographs and also three etchings. He realized happily, "... I have to thank you for etching, I have to thank you for lithography - keep on learning and encourage me more and more to better work ..."

The year 1906 brought several positive changes for Feininger. First he moved to Weimar where he rented a studio in Kurthstrasse 7a. He intended to occupy himself more intensively with graphic work from then on. But one day a "great event" happened: the chief editor of the "Chicago Tribune", the major newspaper in Chicago, visited him in order to contract him. Feininger was to make two pages of comic strips every week. After initial hesitation, he decided to sign the contract, the call from America was too tempting and the income connected with this would be a good basis of existence for his further plans. Apart from this, he was to be allowed a free hand to a great extent in the arrangement, he was not to be told what to do as had been the case with "Ulk". The series "The Kin-der-Kids" and "Wee Willie Winkie's World" which Feininger created for the "Chicago Tribune" became incredibly popular and gained him great respect as an illustrator.

Feininger himself regarded the "contract with Chicago" a "liberation" as it "enabled me to move to Paris and eventually become acquainted with the art world. For the first time I had the chance to think and feel for myself again and to work," he admitted to Alfred Kubin in 1912. He said that he then "found out what art" for him "could and must be."

In Paris he attended - as in 1892/93 - the private art school of the Italian sculptor Filippo Colarossi and was, at the same time, working for the French newspaper "Le Témoin". He also continued to supply "Ulk" and "Lustige Blätter" with drawings.

The French metropolis had much to offer in every respect, it had an atmosphere which hardly anyone could escape, especially not an artist. So fate took its course; the desire to paint grew beyond all bounds in Feininger.

In the Café du Dôme, a meeting place for artists, he made the acquaintance of the German artists Hans Purrmann, Oskar Moll, Rudolf Großmann and Rudolf Levy, who all belonged to a close circle around Henri Matisse. He became friends with Jules Pascin and Robert Delaunay and followed with interest everything which was raised in discussions about artistic views and practices. It did not take him long to make a decision: from then on he would dedicate himself completely to painting.

Feininger cancelled his contracts with the magazines where they had not already run out. The renowned caricaturist risked a new start at 36 years old and began his career as an artist.

It was a logical consequence that suggestions of his previous employment were obvious in his paintings, at first. Figures had been the domain of the illustrator and in the beginning figures dominated the painter's works. His first oil painting: a porcelain monkey on a coloured background.

Feininger felt his way step by step, conquered, with great care, an area which was completely unknown territory to him. He saw himself as a learner and was very self-critical of his actions. He used nature as a pattern although he was not a "nature fanatic" in the negative sense, i.e. he did not think much of "natural colours in the landscape" and later viewed his attempts "to portray nature" as he had done, for example, on a summer holiday in Lobbe on Rügen in 1907 as "dismal things".

However, on the other hand he recognized the benefits which could be drawn from a careful observation of nature, "... The forms which we find new in nature, are newer than anything invented, and only these enrich our fundamental possibility to renew the forms..."

Although Lyonel Feininger had once stated that the sketch was "the soul of art" he was soon able to acquire an insight into the world of colour, to use it, to investigate and reveal it for his purposes. The paintings from 1907 and 1908 already speak an eloquent language with their brilliance of colours.

The artist spent the summer of 1907 in Güntherstal near Freiburg and in Baabe and Lobbe on the island of Rügen where he lived completely withdrawn and was so able to give complete and undivided attention to his new task in hand. On August 28th, he informed Julia, "A great change has come over me... I certainly have learned a lot in a short time, but it was study, they were necessary, meticulously down-to-earth achievements... I look speculatively at my creations - true to scale schoolwork... I want to build on what I have laboriously learned, and try to become more free and independent... it has to become more potent, more broken down and newly formed." And the next day, "... I have completely different light and tone values in my mind - different possibilities of translation - than before, but it is almost impossible to learn the accepted reality. What is seen has to be reformed and crystallized inside..." Of course there were times when he was in doubt about himself and his painting, when he questioned what he had created after a long struggle. However, he did not allow himself to become irritated but continued purposefully on his path and sought other possibilities for solving the problems which arose. In Paris, he got to know paintings by van Gogh and Cézanne, in London works by William Turner. They all made a great impression on him and helped him acquire new knowledge.

In autumn 1908, Feininger moved to Berlin-Zehlendorf with his young wife and the young Andreas. He worked occasionally for "Ulk" and "Lustige Blätter" and a short time later for the "Sporthumor" and the magazine "Licht und Schatten". This was not an inconsistency but came from the necessity of having to look after his family.

In 1910 Feininger exhibited an oil painting for the first time with the Berlin Sezession where he had once before been represented as a draughtsman. In the following year the "Salon des Artistes Indépendants" showed six of his paintings. On the occasion of this exhibition the artist came into contact with works by the French cubists. This encounter was of special interest to Feininger as similar problems of form had occupied him for a long time, "I found the art world excited by cubism. Something I had not heard of, but had sought intuitively for years..."

Feininger now began to take on the form language more intensively than before. Cubism as well as Robert Delaunay's Orphism offered important guidelines, but in no way misled him into being forced into a cubist cliché. "I try to formulate a perspective of the object," he wrote, "which is completely new and completely my own. I would like to place myself in the painting and observe the landscape and the objects which are painted from there."

As usual the individualist in him predominated, and although it cannot be denied that a certain spiritual relationship with the cubists exists, Feininger was able to reinterpret cubism for his personal wishes and concepts and - one could say - to poeticize it. "My cubism, to describe it falsely, as it represents the opposite of the aims of French cubism, is based on the principle of monumentality and concentration to the absolute extremity of my sight . . . my paintings come closer and closer to the synthesis of the fugue . . ."

The connection between his painting and music which Feininger mentions here in his own words was, as it were, a leitmotiv of his art. Even if he chose painting as a profession, it meant in no way that he intended to turn his back forever on the music which had dominated his life until that point. He was always devoutly attached to it and later composed fugues in the spirit of Bach, whose compositions he did not just love but is also supposed to have played exceptionally well on the organ.

"Paintings," he declared, "were almost always a puzzle" to him, "but music" was his "most lively language" which was able to "move him more than any other language". When a musician friend asked him once why he, "in whom Bach was so much a part of his being, had not become a musician instead of a painter," Feininger was able to convince him "that Bach's presence did find expression in his paintings". He could especially have been thinking of his architectural paintings which became a main theme from 1912 and which were, in their construction and rhythm, very much related to Bach's fugues. They could, as it were, be described as painted fugues.

Among the earliest works in this style are "High Buildings I" (1912), "Teltow" (1912) and "Gelmeroda I", the first version of the village church of Gelmeroda, made in 1913. This motif had impressed the artist so much that in later years he returned to it and altogether created thirteen "Gelmeroda"paintings and also numerous sketches, water colours and woodcuts.

In 1913 Lyonel Feininger again moved into his studio in Weimar, from there he searched the Thuringian villages for motifs, sometimes walking, other times on his bicycle. Everything he regarded as suitable in Hopfgarten, Dröbsdorf, Mellingen, Vollersroda, Possendorf, Kleinkromsdorf, Legefeld, Gaberndorf, Denstedt and all the other villages was first of all captured with the pencil. It was to be the "stimulus for many paintings . . . The villages are so old, so derelict and mostly built on such hilly ground that I am favoured with unbelievably fine positions. I make two, three, sometimes four sketches of the same motif, one after the other, until it is captured. I am only able to realize later how valuable these things are . . ."

He was enraptured by the many different impressions, he allowed himself to be carried away by the wealth of subjects which seemed to have been created to excite powers in him that now eventually brought his painting to full blossom, ". . . I can only become human again through painting and have become human again. Whether I like it or not I am subject to this law!... And recently here, in Gelmeroda, in Vollersroda, Mellingen, Taubach, in many places, I have thought of still larger, bolder paintings: soon I will start on them! I had hardly hoped to be able to absorb and work at the same time, but it is the case and it will become stronger and stronger within me. This is surely the first period of maturity in my artistic being. Until now I was only able to make such advancements in drawing. In the last few days, when I worked outside, I literally fell into an ecstasy, towards the end of the afternoon I had become completely instinctive and capable, I stood on the one spot and sketched the same motif three or four times, until I had captured it the way I sensed it. That goes much further than observation or realization, that is the magnetic union, a freeing of all bonds..." (Weimar, May 8th, 1913)

Feininger had already met the artists of "Die Brücke" in 1912; the year 1913 now brought him into contact with the circle around "Der Blaue Reiter". One day he received a letter from Franz Marc in which he was invited to exhibit together with "Der Blaue Reiter" in the "First German Autumn Salon". This was amazing as Feininger had not appeared often as a painter until then. This is why Marc wrote, "... that you have not already received an invitation was because no one in our small circle knew anything about your paintings until Kubin had drawn our attention to them." Feininger and Alfred Kubin had been close friends for a short while. Pleased by Franz Marc's letter he wrote back, "... the letter of invitation arrived exactly on my 42nd birthday - July 17th - and seemed to me to be the most promising present...," and "I cannot conceal the fact from you that my 'being unknown' was, until now, a self-imposed situation so that I could work in peace and with rigid resolution on my development. I am most certainly not at the end of my path..."

But from now on he was no more 'unknown'. Five of his paintings were shown at the "First German Autumn Salon", two of them found buyers in Bernhard Koehler, the important art patron, and in Paul Poiret. The connection to Herwarth Walden and the "Sturm" which was to give such a fruitful co-operation from then on was also founded this way.

In the same year the Munich toy manufacturer Otto Löwenstein commissioned the artist to design trains from painted hardwood for his production line. Feininger who had had a weak spot for trains of every description since his childhood was full of enthusiasm to be able to indulge this love even in more mature years, especially on an artistic level and then on top of this to earn money with it. The letters to his wife - she had remained in Berlin with the children for the time being - witness an untroubled frame of mind. "I am now occupied with the models, I am building really ingenious things, every piece thought out very carefully," he wrote once, for example. On another occasion, "... my model building makes me ... happy, I discover a lot of things in it which I used to like when I was young, the joy in handicraft, the construction and finally the completed playthings!..." He again felt like "the 15-year-old happy boy" and very much hoped that the model trains would be able to bring as much happiness to those for whom they were intended. At the same time he linked great plans with the new task, he wanted to create "an article for the world market" and not just, as was usually the case, "for under the Christmas tree or for one or two years."

Table II

Enchanted Isles. 1942
Watercolour, 30.5 x 37 cm
Städtisches Museum, Mühlheim

After the first patterns were finished and the negotiations with the manufacturer had been completed, the real and partly very complicated work began. This fully occupied the artist so that he wrote to his wife on May 9th, 1914, "I have immediately drawn the necessary conclusions from my inventiveness and commercial actions and have, probably for several weeks, said farewell to painting . . . I . . . have various points to discuss over the most unexpected things which are connected with such a production - labels, box sizes, number and order of waggons per train, technical details etc . . ."

By the middle of June the first parts were "mechanically prefabricated and put together by hand" - as Feininger's son Theodore Lux reported - and the artist was able to begin with the painting of the models. However, the joy only lasted for a short time, the outbreak of World War I forced the manufacture of toys to make way for the production of weapons and munition. Many months' work, the excitement, hopes, wealth of inventiveness and strength which had been invested were destroyed with one blow. The plan was never taken up again. All that remained were several model trains which were later found in the manufacturer's estate after his death.

However, Feininger was much more moved and disturbed by the war as such than by the disappointments which went along with it. He suffered terribly that he was suddenly regarded as an "enemy foreigner" although his sympathies and support still belonged to the country in which he had lived for almost the last thirty years. He wrote in 1915, "Poor Germany! Fights towards its own fall!"

At the outbreak of war he had moved back to Berlin where he sought refuge in his studio and consolation in his painting which had been pushed slightly into the background because of the wooden train project.

Herwarth Walden, the untiring champion where modern art was concerned, succeeded in 1916, in spite of the troubles of the times and the "limitation of freedom of movement" which had been placed on the foreigner Feininger, to arrange an exhibition of works by Lyonel Feininger and Felix Möller in his "Sturm" gallery. In the next year followed - also in "Sturm" - Feininger's first individual show which finally helped him achieve his breakthrough.

In the meantime his artistic ideas had become increasingly clearer, his style more rigid and monumental. Light, space and figures formed a unit. He had recognized and solved all problems which were connected with space, proportion, colour and perspective. Later he explained to his son, looking back: "When I began to paint in 1907, I was just a cartoonist and my aims in oil painting were unclear. The only possibility seemed to me to be the poster. Or to express it less clearly, my ideal was to build up pictures from coloured silhouettes . . . I also remembered the impression which certain shooting gallery figures had made on me. They were made of tin and were really primitive and painted with violent colours with no shadowing . . . Light and shadow and whatever else one can include in a painting to create an atmospheric effect will alone never reach the final aim in painting which is based on spatial relationships. In modern art . . . it is mainly the placement of the special structure which is essential and goes before all other pictorial elements. This division of space has to be reduced as logically as possible to the greatest possible simplification of all parts. Simple and generous areas of colour, bound together on the canvas - this should be the aim . . ."

When Feininger turned his attention to the woodcut in 1918, this was at first because of external difficulties. At this point in time it was almost impossible to find paints or other painting utensils, and when they existed they were of such poor quality that they were out of the question for an artist's standards. Therefore Feininger made a virtue of necessity - as did several of his colleagues - and turned to the woodcut. It did not take him long to become an expert in this field as well. One can see how enthusiastically he worked in this area by the fact that he had made more than 300 woodcuts, 117 of which were created within the first year.

After times had become better and better quality materials were available again, Feininger preferred to use expensive handmade paper from Japan because it brought out the black and white contrasts stronger and more expressively than other paper. The topics which he chose for his woodcuts were the same as he favoured in his oil paintings: architecture, sea, navy and sailing boats. The sailing ships reached their first peak in the woodcuts from 1918/19.

In 1919 the architect Walter Gropius founded the "Bauhaus" in Weimar. This was an institution which came from the union of art academy and arts-and-crafts school and was to be cultivated in the co-operation between art, industry and trade. In the manifesto, which Gropius drew up and which carried on the front page Lyonel Feininger's woodcut "Cathedral of Socialism", it said, "The Bauhaus endeavours to collect all artistic creations to one unit, the reunification of all artistic disciplines - sculpture, painting, arts-and-crafts and skilled trade - with a new style of architecture as their integral component. The final, if distant, aim is the unified work of art - the great building - in which there is no border between monumental and decorative art..."

Famous artists were commissioned as "form masters" to lead the individual workshops, master craftsmen were available to answer all relevant technical questions, and social aspects were to be considered by the renewal of form. The medieval masonic lodge, a workshop community of stonemasons, who were employed in the building of a large church, served as a pattern. In both cases the complete work of art stood in the foreground.

Feininger was the first artist whom Gropius appointed as master in the "Bauhaus". Others included Paul Klee, Wassily Kandinsky, Oskar Schlemmer, Georg Muche, Gerhard Marcks, László Moholy-Nagy, Johannes Itten, Josef Albers and Herbert Bayer. Personalities whose names alone could guarantee valuable artistic and art-pedagogic work. There was a great deal of solidarity among the masters. Since everyone knew the capabilities of the other, there was mutual respect. In fact lasting friendships developed over and above the respect which each of them had for his colleague. Lyonel Feininger had especially close contact to Kandinsky, Klee, Muche and Marcks. In the Bauhaus, Feininger was in charge of the printing workshop, Gerhard Marcks of the pottery and Georg Muche of the weaving workshop. Kandinsky taught in the mural studio and Klee in the glass painting workshop.

We can thank the painter, architect and Bauhaus colleague Georg Muche for a characteristic of Feininger's from this time which brings the artist as well as the person closer to us. "In the Bauhaus, Feininger was the example for the mysterious workings of a man who creates quietly from the depths, of an artist who is at peace with himself and radiates. No one was able to evade this inobtrusive effect which challenged no one to contradiction and only evoked goodness. In this sense there could be no educational methods, no artistic training with accepted standards by which he would have been able to convince. He taught unintentionally through his own example as a person and graphic artist.

There are many people who remember a visit to his studio. They were so strongly impressed that the memories are still as vivid decades later because Feininger's words had become decisively important to them. One should not think that Feininger gave the impression of being a hermit, who was sure of his mission in life. He could be childishly happy and was at the same time clever and well-versed in many subjects. He loved cheerful games in the circle of his three sons just as much as music and literature. He composed fugues and played them on the harmonium which stood in his studio. Once I saw how a Bauhaus pupil came to him and proudly told that he had examined Kandinsky's, Klee's and Feininger's paintings according to the rules of the harmonic progression and the golden section and that a painting of Feininger's was composed in a magnificent way to the rules of the golden section. Feininger smiled and laughed at him. He was full of amazement and joy at this successful trick of chance and at the bringer of this information. It awakened his sense for the grotesque, his enjoyment of clowns and circus. On tables around stood his hand-carved locomotives and trains giving the impression of speed frozen for the moment, beside those lay the streamlined sailing boat models which he had built in Deep on the Baltic Sea and had tested in regattas. He took one of three linnets which had flown in through his window in a snowstorm that day and which he had overfed with hemp so that they were intoxicated and dazed. He said to the young artist, 'Do you not think that this linnet is also constructed according to the golden section? It looks as if it is and knows nothing about it. And neither do I!'"

Feininger never made a great fuss about himself. He remained modest, never acted as if he was the great expert nor presumed upon his authority as a teacher. On the contrary, he treated his pupils as equals, and they thanked him for it with loyalty and devotion. Although he had been appointed as professor by the central government, Feininger refused to be addressed by this title either privately or in public. He just wanted to be what he was, the painter and graphic artist Lyonel Feininger.

In this phase of his activities a great sense of peace spread over his work. Paintings were made which can be reckoned as being among his most beautiful - filled with light and transparency, simple and direct in their form, cheerful and lyrical in their atmosphere. Paintings as for example "The Studio Window" (1919), "Groß-Kromsdorf" (1921), "Architecture II" (1921) or "Beleuchtete Häuser" (Lit up Houses) (1921).

The Thuringian landscape was a continuing source of fascination for Feininger. "This is my country!" he said once and described Weimar as the city of his "life's wonder". Inspired by the lovely surroundings in which he lived, he turned increasingly to water colours in those years as well as sketches, woodcuts and oil painting. "... In an extremely sensitive union of soft sketches which only suggest the most necessary contours with colouring kept to a few areas, he created dreamlike, unmistakable, individual works, witness to his aristocratic, sensitive artistic personality..." (Per Amann)

In 1924 Feininger, Kandinsky, Klee and Jawlensky founded the group "Die Blaue Vier", and together they organized a series of exhibitions, for example, in New York, Chicago, on the American West Coast and in Mexico.

Two years later, the Weimar period of the Bauhaus came to an end. Since its foundation the institution had been open to criticism and hostility from anti-republican parties. The more successful the Bauhaus was from a cultural viewpoint, the greater was the malevolence from certain political circles. "The opposition used, as well as the usual means such as refusing money and placing votes of no confidence in central parliamentary members who favoured the Bauhaus, also the less pleasant forms such as slander and the spreading of vicious rumours," reported Lyonel Feininger's youngest son. "My father as well as all the other masters was often drawn into discussions with unfriendly government representatives in the hope that after they had seen the place they would be able to realize that the Bauhaus was neither a hothouse of anarchy nor a breeding ground for free love and not even an asylum for criminal madness. Studios and workshops were, in recurring periods, open to the unwilling guests who, in answer to Gropius's energetic and clearly presented commentaries as to the continuation of work, either ignored him completely or replied with tactless and inappropriate counterquestions. While this resistance, which demonstrated all variations of open attack to subversive intrigue, strengthened the loyalty of masters and students to their ideal, the final political result is well-known. Less than seven years after the hopeful beginnings they left the city of Weimar with a sigh of relief."

Feininger moved with the Bauhaus to Dessau where - until the final closure by the National Socialists - he carried on working as form master, however, at his own request without having to teach from then on.

Walter Gropius stepped down as director in 1928, his successor Hans Meyer remained just two years in office. Ludwig Mies van der Rohe, who took over the directorship in 1930 under the most unfavourable conditions, tried hard to prevent the dissolution, but in spite of untiring dedication it was in vain. His plan to carry on the Bauhaus after its closure in Dessau as a private institute in a former telephone factory in Berlin had to remain a dream because of the political situation.

Seen as a whole, the years which Lyonel Feininger spent in the Bauhaus were a time of fruitful creation, artistic maturity and development, a time in which the experiences which he gained as tutor and form master enriched his art. Above all, however, the activities in the Bauhaus offered him the opportunity of realizing something which had always been close to his heart: he could be useful to society.

However, doubts as to his own ability remained, he was alternately satisfied, then dissatisfied with himself and his work. ". . . My own artistic works are the battle-ground where I have to overcome myself and eliminate everything conflicting to achieve harmony and unity," he once said. The more famous he became, the greater were the demands which he placed on himself, and it made no difference if he was dealing with a large or a small work, an important or less important work. He devoted all his love and attention to even the smallest composition and worked at it so long until his requirements were met. ". . . My little painting has risen for the last time, and this time from a terrible chaos, now it really is there and will be good . . . I have learned to paint again for the hundredth time on this silly little painting. One does not see what a struggle and tenacity of will is necessary for such a small canvas . . ."

Feininger was just as honest in his letters as he sincerely attempted to be with himself. With no palliation he described his conflicts, and time and time again

Table III

Lit up Houses. 1921
Watercolour, 20.5 x 29.8 cm
Kunstmuseum, Düsseldorf

accused himself of artistic failure and weakness, on the other side he expressed his joy at developments and new knowledge. These documents are invaluable not least because of this frankness. We, who know and love his art, can hardly understand why an artist like him could think he could "not measure up" to others and assume a "certain narrow-mindedness" in his own works, however, one can imagine many of the things which he mentions in his letters and understand them. Together with his artistic works they help to create a full picture of Lyonel Feininger's personality. The following example also allows us a glimpse into the artist's workshop. ". . . I work very freely . . . and continue my summer work in colour, almost as freely improvised as the charcoal sketches," he wrote in 1927. "There is a fresh and powerful feeling for form in it; the constructed, frozen form has become more lively, suffers and even seeks refractions . . . I know what I am looking for and am satisfied . . . I am getting on well, and it will continue so. I have painted several times till ten o'clock in the evening under artificial light, these hours were very valuable . . . in these days I bring all my strength together, destroy and build, without this cycle painting remains tentative and unsatisfactory. Until now the plus was on the building side . . . It is too long since I 'fought' while painting, now it seems to work. I hate these half measures from the last weeks . . . sometimes one falls in love too soon with the nascent which has to die several deaths before life is breathed, drummed, thundered in (as the case may be) . . ."

One recognizes confidence in these words. The way seemed clear, the target he was seeking seemed close. But appearances are deceptive. It did not take long before he admitted to his son, "I am working, but worse than ever before - when I often made bad paintings in earlier years they were always dictated by desire and self-confidence - and now the whole person Feininger is a question mark and a doubt. This condition will pass, I am sure of it . . ."

Lack of courage on one hand, hope and confidence on the other. The ups and downs of his moods were just as characteristic for Feininger as his iron will, the driving force which in spite of everything never waned.

When he worked again on old paintings, which was often the case, he did not do it just because he felt such a retouching to be necessary, but because this activity seemed to him "very informative". He was so best able to judge the development which his art had made in the meantime.

One of Feininger's idiosyncracies was that he divided his work into summer and winter work, i.e. during the summer which he preferred to spend in the country, especially in Heringsdorf and Deep, he created aquarelles, in winter oil paintings. The strict division of the two fields first came about because he did not want to carry around heavy and unmanageable working utensils with him on his summer stays. However, he soon noticed that this method also had some good in it in other respects, that it brought him valuable "knowledge" and because of this he kept it.

Feininger was what one could call an intelligent artist, and because of this he had a great variety of artistic and technical media at his disposal. He loved variations. Motifs which had fascinated him once never let go of him. "Gelmeroda", "Zirchow", "Paddle-Steamer", "The Red Tower", "Gaberndorf" or "Groß-Kromsdorf" run through his oeuvre for many years. They return time and time again with a different countenance.

". . . whether oil painting or water colour, etching or woodcut, also within each of these techniques there is always a wealth of possibilities. Soon he drew sharp geometric lines with the ruler, soon he worked with nervous, shaky lines. Once the pictures are composed from small, sharp forms, another time from large simple areas. Often nothing but cool, blue, green, grey tones dominate the canvas, then again there are bright reds or shining yellows. In many paintings and prints the forms push and press closely and tightly, in others order is formed with the most economical media, through a few points, lines or surfaces . . ." (Alfred Hentzen)

In spite of this variety, Feininger's handwriting remained unmistakable - in its endeavour towards "de-materialization" and "transfiguration", clear in its form, transparent in the colours, atmospheric and original in its expression.

The artist often sought seclusion in order to be able to work without any distractions, away from the hustle and bustle. It was a desire and at the same time a necessity, but after weeks and months of extreme concentration and tension there was always the moment when being alone started to depress him. Then he revived himself in his family circle and dedicated himself to building model sailing boats whose seaworthiness he tested out together with his three sons during holidays on the river Rega. He proudly watched "how the little things tacked against the waves which were much higher than the tips of the masts". He constantly reformed and improved until every boat had become a "perfect, trustworthy, high-class 'physical' tool". He was not content with half-measures in this activity either, and still it served as relaxation and created the necessary balance. ". . . Otherwise one never experienced that I could really relax from my work for a time - but with this occupation with the boats I really do rest for a while . . ."

Since his taking part in the "First German Autumn Salon" in 1913 the art world had shown him its admiration with respect and acknowledgement. He had been represented in countless exhibitions since then as, for example, in Dresden, Weimar, Wroclaw, Magdeburg, Erfurt, Hanover, Munich, Düsseldorf and Basel, but also in New York, San Francisco and Los Angeles and at the XVII Biennial in Venice. In 1931 Berlin honoured him on the occasion of his sixtieth birthday with an exhibition in the Kronprinzenpalais.

From 1929 - 1931 the artist always spent part of the year in Halle where he had been commissioned by the council to paint a cityscape which was to be a present for the senior presiding committee in Magdeburg. The city fathers went to great expense to enable Feininger to have optimum working conditions. This shows the importance of this task. In the "Red Tower" on the Giebichenstein they had furnished him a studio in one of the tower rooms with several windows, in which he could work undisturbed when he stayed there. Aloys Schardt, the director of the Municipal Moritzburg Museum of Halle, can be thanked for the fact that Feininger painted this picture. He was a great admirer of the artist and had done his utmost to see that Feininger was chosen.

Feininger involved himself fully in this task, it was just the right thing to evoke his passion. ". . . The start of spring! The sky full of violins! In the tower I stand in front of the open window from morning till night and paint, and every brushstroke 'sits', everything around me is colourful and an unprecedented joy . . . It is strange how I am suddenly a new person here - the colourfulness, the atmosphere, my room, everything supports me and inspires me, the concentration is so complete . . . It was worth after having been dead for so many months to be able to experience this condition again . . ."

Fascinated by the splendour which his artist's eye experienced when he looked out of the windows, he literally fell into a creative frenzy so that when he was finished there was not just one view of Halle but eleven paintings and twenty-eight drawings which were all bought by the Moritzburg Museum and count among the most important works by the artist.

While Feininger - cut off from his surroundings - dedicated himself to this great task, a catastrophe in the political sector slowly developed, the dimensions of which no one could imagine then. The worldwide economic crisis also left its mark on Germany, and so, in the false hope of better times, the way was evened for a course of politics whose radical methods finally led to complete ruin.

Very soon after the National Socialists' seizure of power, Feininger was made to realize that the policy of art politics which was now practised was nothing more than a declaration of war against anyone who did not work correspondingly to the spirit of the age, and that under the circumstances no more constructive work would be possible in the long run. First he sought refuge in Deep where he had so often spent happy summer months. There he was able to feel relatively free and could develop artistically in complete seclusion. But this idyll was destroyed when the political situation worsened.

As Feininger had been asked to lead a summer course in Mills College in Oakland, California, he travelled again to America on May 6th, 1936. His return to Germany brought home the painful discovery that a future in the country which had been a spiritual and artistic home to him for fifty years was out of the question. With a heavy heart the 66 year old Feininger decided to burn his boats and move to the United States for ever. This decision was all the more difficult to make as he was a famous artist in Germany, but in America he was relatively unknown. It meant he more or less had to start all over again.

It was no wonder that he suddenly felt completely foreign and uprooted. In Germany he had been regarded as an American, in America it was the other way round: people saw in him a German artist, which of course had a bad tinge to it at that time. It was not easy for him to come to terms "spiritually, professionally and economically". At last in 1939 - Feininger had already been there for two years - he again found the time to paint. "Now it does not hurt anymore when I am described as 'the German painter'. In the beginning I suffered terribly under the feeling of being foreign. But now," he wrote to his son Theodore Lux on June 27th, 1939, "I only feel the incredible advantage which exists because I lived so long in Europe. My work draws its impetus from there."

Of course he was under no illusions: It could take a considerable time until he could find buyers for his paintings. Until then he just had to contain himself, have patience and not lose courage. According to a description by the youngest son, Feininger and his wife lived in New York in the beginning "almost in poverty". No one wanted to buy anything, and a newspaper to which he had sent several photographs and reproductions of paintings rejected them with the comment that they were sorry but they were too "subtle" for the reader.

There was nothing left for the artist but to seek a way out of this situation. He found this, taking into account the economic situation in the modern art market, he was willing to make concessions in the price of his paintings. In a letter from June 25th, 1941 he wrote, "I can report good news again. Yesterday two very pleasant and enthusiastic letters arrived from museums in San Diego. The one stated that two water colours were bought by museums for 125 dollars (my reduced price); the other said that an aquarelle in the exhibition in San Diego had received an 'honourable mention'. This impressed the director, Dr. Poland, so much that he wrote me a nice letter about it, informing me at the same time how little money the museums have at the present . . . The buying commission . . . was very sorry that it could only buy two of my drawings, asked me, however, if I would possibly be prepared to 'round off the purchase' by giving a third aquarelle as a gift to the collection which would be permanently exhibited in the museum. I think that in this special case the drawing which Poland requested (a small abstract ship, listed at 50 dollars) would be an enrichment to the group and certainly would be well placed, better than unseen and unappreciated in my portfolio at home. I have therefore decided to place it on the 'advertising budget' . . ."

The first step was made, the American public became interested in Feininger's work. And then came, overnight as it were, the main turning-point, the final breakthrough. In the art exhibition "Artists of Victory" in 1942 in the Metropolitan Museum of Art, Feininger won the buying price for his painting "Gelmeroda XII". He described himself how it came about. "Yesterday I went to the 'varnishing' (as the people still call it) of the new exhibition of American painting in the Metropolitan Museum, as one of my paintings is included . . . Dr. L. took it there himself, although the date for delivery was already past (as I do not belong to the 'inner circle' I had not received an invitation to take part). The exhibition was meant to represent the victory of the American artist, and after the three thousand paintings had been reduced to three hundred by a preliminary jury, and these had been hung and presented to the dear old public, a second jury was to decide which of these works were to be bought by the Metropolitan . . . Dear me, was I disheartened as . . . I saw the hordes of people . . . but nevertheless I found my 'Gelmeroda' (now modestly entitled 'Church') hung very nicely . . ."

He reckoned the chances of it being numbered among the chosen few as "one to ten thousand", but when he noticed that with the exception of a "corpulent, unfashionable looking lady" no one obviously took any notice of the painting, his hopes melted, low as they already were, to almost zero. His surprise was so much greater when he received a registered letter from the Metropolitan Museum the next morning. ". . . Hm, I thought; . . . but when I saw the contents I almost fell down . . . a cheque for 2.500 dollars lay in my hand, tout comme ça . . ."

From then on events followed in quick succession, Feininger was honoured in every way one could think of, and - the irony of fate - although before, as a German artist he had hardly been given any attention, it was, in an exhibition of American painting, a German motif which won the heart of the viewer and helped its creator to becoming honoured in America.

Feininger was moved by the show of affection and good will which friends, colleagues and art dealers accorded him. But more than all the appreciation, the feeling of eventually being at home in America, being accepted by his fellow

Table IV

Vision of a Small Sailing Boat. 1935
Watercolour on paper, 30 x 41 cm
Kaiser Wilhelm Museum, Krefeld

countrymen as belonging to them, played a great part in his inner contentment and fired his creative power. "The artist had taken his place," was the opinion of his son Theodore Lux. "After society held back its appreciation no longer - after they had made good the long hesitation with true American generosity - we will soon be able to observe the artist in his productive and strong 'late period' . . ."

This "late period", Feininger's "graphic period", commenced with a series of Manhattan pictures. More intensively than before, he now directed his attention towards everything atmospheric, used more than ever before the interaction of fog and light in his work, and so when one talks of his "graphic period", the field of graphic printing is not meant but rather the structure of his paintings and water colours. "I tend more and more to reduce my statements to the purest essence of line and colour in painting; as a painter I feel hopelessly bound although I know in my own small way how to appreciate the properties of pigments. I am coming close to a stage in which I actually begin to destroy the precise form, in favour of - at least it seems to me - the uniformity. This is a precarious stage which I enter, and occasionally something stops me going still further; then as compensation I turn to some contradiction . . ."

In 1943 Feininger won the Worcester Museum of Art prize. 1944 the New York Museum of Modern Art organized the first large exhibition of his works. He was now famous in America as well, his art had also succeeded here.

In 1945 he again began his teaching activities and held a summer course in the Black Mountain College in North Carolina. After this he travelled to Stockbridge, Massachusetts, where he regularly spent the summer months until 1948.

In 1947 the 76 year old Feininger was honoured by being elected as president of the "Federation of American Painters and Sculptors". Exhibitions in many states of America spread his art in the whole country and Feininger never became tired of adding new works to those already existing. During a stay in Plymouth he wrote, "In the evenings I truly enjoy beginning a sketch which can then be worked on by daylight. I must admit it is mainly droll figures which give me the opportunity to work with bright colours . . . I have also taken colour photographs here (in Plymouth, Mass.) . . . I mainly like these yellow hydrants with red heads and black service pipes . . . they are at least pure colours. What I miss the most is drawing from nature, making 'notes' as I used to on the Baltic, in Deep or in the villages in the Weimar surroundings. Somehow the motifs here give me no satisfaction; they play such a small part in my inner preferences and lead to nothing more than naturalistic exercises."

Although Feininger had found a new home, the yearning for the once long-familiar was so deeply imbedded that he was unable to do anything else but to allow the memories of those places to come alive again and again over thousands of miles - in his heart as well as in his paintings.

When in 1950 the first Feininger exhibition in Germany after the war was planned by the Kestner organization in Hanover the artist was very pleased. "In the gallery we are preparing material for my forthcoming exhibition in Germany. I am . . . very happy about the fact that this exhibition is taking place. It is a sort of 'vindication' and actually an 'expression of thanks' to many friends over there."

It was a great success and because of this was also shown in Paris - the first Feininger exhibition there - in Munich, Brunswick, Mannheim, Düsseldorf, Hamburg and Berlin and - as the first Feininger exhibition in Britain - in York, Cambridge and London.

It did not take long before the "Bavarian Academy of Fine Arts" organized a new exhibition of his works. "From Germany I receive superlatives from critics of the Munich exhibition," he said in 1954, "They are, above all, held in tones of personal cordiality; all the headings include the words 'Reunion with Feininger'. And one can see the intention to make amends for previous unsettled scores."

With unbroken strength and undiminished ambition Feininger, who was over eighty years old, continued to work at his task in life. He created oil paintings such as "Phoenix" (1954), "Composition: Gable VI" (1954) and "Evening Haze" (1955) or water colours such as "Blue Village Church" (1955) and "Village with Figures" (1955) to name a few. Intensity, concentration and resourcefulness remained with him to the end. ". . . I will not be talked into accepting that the time has finally come when one can be satisfied with weakening," he wrote to Karl Schmidt-Rottluff ten days before his death.

On January 13th, 1956 a rich artistic life came to an end. Feininger died in New York, the city of his birth. He equally represented German and American art. "The question as to whether German or American is only important if contributing to the understanding of Lyonel Feininger's art. Nationalities lose their sense here. However, language and climate in a spiritual as well as in a meteorological sense are very important. A great art speaks from a great spirit. And great is who absorbs an inherited quality from East and West and changes it up to a higher level." (Theodore Lux Feininger)

Feininger was one of these great people. His spirit lives on in his work, his language is understood by everyone, because it is a language that knows no borders and needs no words.

ILLUSTRATIONS

The White Man. 1907
Oil on canvas, 68 x 55 cm
Thyssen-Bornemisza Collection, Lugano

Street in Paris. 1909

Oil on canvas, 100 x 81.4 cm
The University of Iowa Museum of Art, Iowa

The Great Revolution. 1910

Oil on canvas, 104.4 x 95.4 cm
Museum of Modern Art, New York
Gift of Mrs. Julia Feininger

On the Quay. 1912
Oil on canvas, 40.4 x 48,5 cm
Sprengel Museum, Hanover

Bicycle Race. 1912

Oil on canvas, 80 x 100 cm
Private collection

Fishing Fleet in Swell. 1912

Oil on canvas, 40.5 x 48.5 cm
Sprengel Museum, Hanover

Light Beacon. 1913

Oil on canvas, 100 x 80 cm
Museum Folkwang, Essen

Umpferstedt. 1914
Oil on canvas, 131.5 x 101 cm
Kunstmuseum Nordrhein-Westfalen, Düsseldorf

Head with Large Green Eyes. 1915
Oil on canvas, 70 x 62 cm
Private collection

41

Marine. 1914/1915

Oil on canvas, 60 x 75 cm
Galerie Nierendorf, West Berlin

Green Bridge II. 1916

Oil on canvas, 125 x 100 cm
North Carolina Museum of Art, Raleigh
Gift of Mrs. Ferdinand Möller

Still Life with Jugs. 1916

Oil on canvas, 80 x 100 cm
Kunstmuseum, Düsseldorf

47

Studio Window. 1918

Oil on canvas, 100 x 80 cm
Wilhelm-Lehmbruck-Museum, Duisburg

Mellingen Church. 1920
Oil on canvas, 60.5 x 75.5 cm
Von der Heydt-Museum, Wuppertal

Architecture II. 1921

Oil on canvas, 100 x 78.7 cm
Thyssen-Bornemisza Collection, Lugano

Oberweimar. 1921

Oil on canvas, 80 x 100 cm
Museum Boymans van Beuningen, Rotterdam

Groß-Kromsdorf III. 1921

Oil on canvas, 100 x 80 cm
The Harward University Art Museum
Buch-Reisinger Museum, Cambridge
Gift of Mrs. Julia Feininger

Tower I. 1923/1926

Oil on canvas, 61 x 47.5 cm
Kunstmuseum, Basel

Tower II. 1925
Oil on canvas, 100 x 80 cm
Kunsthalle, Karlsruhe

Schooner on the Baltic Sea. 1924

Oil on canvas, 40.5 x 23.8 cm
Private collection

Tower I. 1923/1926

Oil on canvas, 61 x 47.5 cm
Kunstmuseum, Basel

Tower II. 1925
Oil on canvas, 100 x 80 cm
Kunsthalle, Karlsruhe

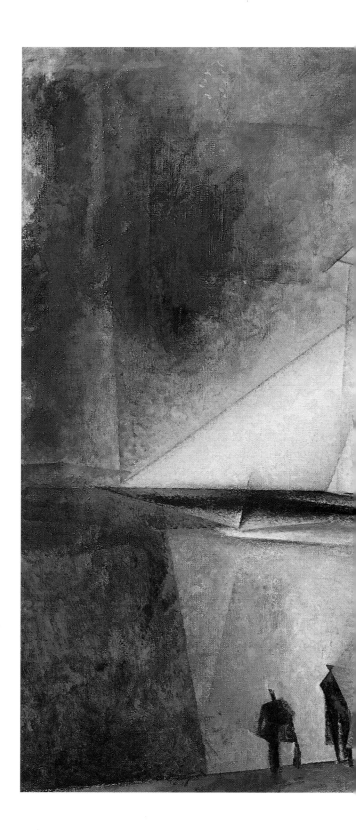

Victory of the Sloop Mary. 1926

Oil on canvas, 21.5 x 33.5 cm
St. Louis Art Museum, St. Louis

71

Gelmeroda IX. 1926

Oil on canvas, 108 x 80 cm
Museum Folkwang, Essen

Marine. 1927

Oil on canvas, 55 x 90 cm
Marlborough Fine Art, London

The Grütz Tower in Treptow on the River Rega. 1928
Oil on canvas, 101.3 x 81 cm
Hessisches Landesmuseum, Darmstadt

The Mouth of the Rega III. 1929

Oil on canvas, 48 x 77 cm
Kunsthalle, Hamburg

Halle, 'Am Trödel'. 1929

Oil on canvas, 100 x 80 cm
Bauhaus-Archiv Museum, West Berlin

Yachts. 1929
Oil on canvas, 46.3 x 72.4 cm
Staatsgalerie, Stuttgart

Market Church in Halle. 1930

Oil on canvas, 102 x 80.4 cm
Bayerische Staatsgemäldesammlung, Munich

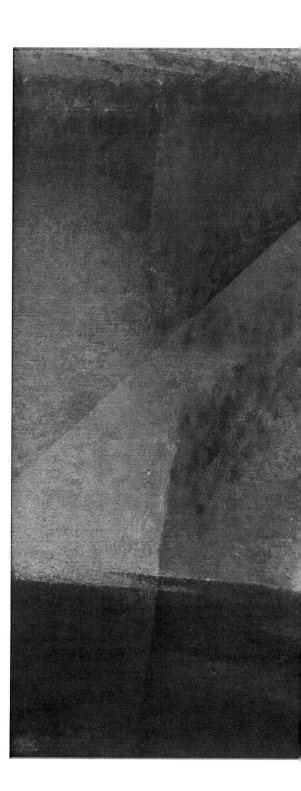

Pyramide of Sails. 1930
Oil on canvas, 46.3 x 73 cm
Private collection

East Choir of the Cathedral in Halle. 1931
Oil on canvas, 100 x 80 cm
Kunsthalle, Hamburg

Lit Row of Houses. 1932

Oil on canvas, 43.5 x 72.5 cm
Kunstmuseum, Basel

The Red Violinist. 1934

Oil on canvas, 100 x 80 cm
Private collection

Houses in New York. 1945

Oil on canvas, 40.5 x 58.5 cm
Marlborough Gallery, New York

Dark Gaberndorf. 1946

Oil on canvas, 71 x 89 cm
Marlborough Gallery, New York

Queen of Hudson. 1947

Oil on canvas, 35.5 x 71 cm
Marlborough Gallery, New York

Shadow of Dissolution. 1953

Oil on canvas, 91.5 x 76.2 cm
Private collection

101

Rue Saint Jacques, Paris. 1953

Oil on canvas, 91 x 71 cm
Marlborough Gallery, New York

103

105

108

116

120

131

Feininger · Dröbsdorf · Sonnt. d. 7. Okt. 1923

feininger   22 vii 51

TABLE OF ILLUSTRATIONS

Rainy Day at the Beach. 1918
Woodcut, 13.6 x 21.4 cm
Print 1 from the portfolio 'Twelve Woodcuts' 1921

Town with Church in the Sun. 1918
Woodcut, 16.4 x 24.7 cm
Print 4 from the portfolio 'Twelve Woodcuts' 1921

Windmill in Werder. 1918
Woodcut, 17.9 x 17.9 cm

Ship-Owners Taking a Walk. 1918
Woodcut, 37 x 29.5 cm

Train on the Bridge. 1918
Woodcut, 9.2 x 11.6 cm
Print 3 from the portfolio 'Twelve Woodcuts' 1921

Daasdorf. 1918
Woodcut, 33 x 45 cm

Ships in the Harbour. 1918
Woodcut, 8.2 x 11.8 cm

Sailing Boats. 1918
Woodcut, 28 x 37.7 cm

Gelmeroda with Fir Tree
Woodcut, 21.8 x 17.3 cm
Print 5 from the portfolio 'Twelve Woodcuts' 1921

Gelmeroda. 1918
Woodcut, 28.5 x 23.2 cm

Village Church Benz VI. 1919
Woodcut, 20 x 26.2 cm

Church with Tower and Apsis. 1919
Woodcut, 25.4 x 30.4 cm

Zottelstedt. 1919
Woodcut, 32 x 40.5 cm

Troistedt. 1919
Woodcut, 17.2 x 22.1 cm

Windmill. 1919
Woodcut, 25.5 x 30.5 cm

High Sailing Boats. 1919
Woodcut, 19.1 x 25 cm

111 top

111 bottom

112

113

114 top

114 bottom

115 top

115 bottom

116

117

118 top

118 bottom

119 top

119 bottom

120

121

Cruising Sailing Boats. 1919
Woodcut, 17.1 x 22.5 cm

122 top

Ready for Departure. 1919
Woodcut, 17.5 x 21.3 cm
Print 7 from the portfolio 'Twelve Woodcuts' 1921

122 bottom

Navy Fleet. 1919
Woodcut, 16.6 x 23.5 cm
Print 8 from the portfolio 'Twelve Woodcuts' 1921

123 top

Cruising Sailing Boats. 1919
Woodcut, 22.5 x 30 cm

123 bottom

Houses in Paris. 1919
Woodcut, 31.2 x 25.5 cm

124

Mellingen. 1919
Woodcut, 30.4 x 25.4 cm

125

Church in the Forest. 1920
Woodcut, 14.3 x 11.5 cm
Print 10 from the portfolio 'Twelve Woodcuts' 1921

126 top

Ships on the Shore. 1920
Woodcut, 10.5 x 16.2 cm

126 bottom

Ships on the Rocky Beach. 1920
Woodcut, 12 x 15.3 cm

127 top

Tahiti. 1920
Woodcut, 16.3 x 18.8 cm
Print 12 from the portfolio 'Twelve Woodcuts' 1921

127 bottom

Gelmeroda. 1920
Woodcut, 23.4 x 24.8 cm

128

Houses in Paris. 1920
Woodcut, 37.3 x 27.1 cm

129

Village with Square in the Foreground
Woodcut, 21.6 x 34.2 cm

130 top

Architecture. 1920
Woodcut, 15.5 x 22.6 cm
Print 11 from the portfolio 'Twelve Woodcuts' 1921

130 bottom

Zirchow. 1920
Woodcut, 20.3 x 24.5 cm

131 top

At the Jetty Wall. 1921
Woodcut, 16.7 x 21.8 cm

131 bottom

Dröbsdorf. 1923   132 top
Ink drawing, 28 x 37 cm
Bauhaus-Archiv, West Berlin

Suburb I. 1924   132 bottom
Woodcut, 23.6 x 37.6 cm

St. Mary's Church in Halle   133
Charcoal drawing, 40.3 x 29.7 cm
Museum Folkwang, Essen

Paris IV. 1931   134
Chalk drawing, 30.2 x 23.5 cm
Galerie Nierendorf, West Berlin

Yellow Village Church III. 1931   135 top
Woodcut, 18.9 x 22.6 cm

Small Locomotive. 1936   135 bottom
Woodcut, 5.2 x 8.5 cm

Lüneburg. 1951   136
Pen drawing, 38.7 x 31.5 cm
Galerie Nierendorf, West Berlin

Reproduction rights Lyonel Feininger: © COSSMOPRESS, Geneva, 1988

Photographic acknowledgements:
Colorphoto Hans Hins SWB, CH-Allschwil: P. 63, 67, 91
Fotostudio R. Kleinhempel, Hamburg: P. 79, 89
Artothek J. Hinrichs, Planegg: P. 93

The publishers wish to thank the respective museums and galleries for allowing the use of photographic material on
the following pages:
p. 25, 27, 29, 31, 43, 45, 49, 51, 53, 57, 59, 61, 69, 81, 83, 105, 107, 108, 109, 110, 111, 112, 114 top, 115 top, 116, 119 bottom,
120, 122 bottom, 123 top, 126, 127, 130 bottom, 131 top, 132, 133, 134, 135, 136.
All other reproductions where no source is mentioned are taken from the Berghaus archives.